MW01120840

TO:

FROM:

the**Coupon**Collection™

SOURCEBOOKS, INC.®
NAPERVILLE, ILLINOIS

The Perfect

VIRGO
Coupons

A coupon gift to inspire
the best in you

 SOURCEBOOKS, INC.®
NAPERVILLE, ILLINOIS

Copyright © 2004 by Sourcebooks, Inc.
Cover and internal design © 2004 by Sourcebooks, Inc.
Cover and internal illustration © 2004 Anne Crosse
Sourcebooks and the colophon are registered trademarks of Sourcebooks, Inc.

All rights reserved. No part of this book may be reproduced in any form or by any electronic or mechanical means including information storage and retrieval systems—except in the case of brief quotations embodied in critical articles or reviews—without permission in writing from its publisher, Sourcebooks, Inc.

Published by Sourcebooks, Inc.
P.O. Box 4410, Naperville, Illinois 60567-4410
(630) 961-3900
FAX: (630) 961-2168
www.sourcebooks.com

ISBN 1-4022-0187-7

Printed and bound in the United States of America

AP 10 9 8 7 6 5 4 3 2 1

THE PERFECT VIRGO

Born August 23 – September 22

Welcome to the world of the perfect Virgo. Astrology is a powerful symbolic language for describing and interpreting human life and events on the Earth. This coupon book is a fun way to dip into that ancient pool of knowledge and make the most of the potential that lies in your nature.

WHY ASTROLOGY?

Astrologers believe that the makeup, configuration, and movement of the planets and stars correspond with events anywhere in the universe, including human lives, and that studying these cycles can help people understand the past and present, and even predict the future. By mapping the position of the other planets in our galaxy, the moon, and the sun in the heavens when you were born, astrology finds indications of the circumstances you may encounter, as well as clues to your basic personality traits and how you relate to others.

THE TWELVE HOUSES

Imagine a wheel in space that circles the Earth like a cigar band. This band is divided into twelve sections, or houses, because the sun spends approximately one month in each area in relationship to the Earth, as our planet makes its yearly journey around the sun. (In ancient times, of course, it was believed that the sun was, in fact, circling the Earth.) The wheel of the Zodiac divides the heavens into the twelve traditional astrological groupings, each of which is assigned certain polarities, qualities, and elements. The Zodiac wheel also makes clear the relationships among the signs. For instance, Virgo is located on the wheel directly opposite the sign of Pisces, and is in many ways the Fish's opposite in values and interests.

Although the location of the sun at the time of your birth—your sun sign—provides the basic key to your personality, in astrology, *each* of the planets in our galaxy, as well as the moon, has influences which are expressed in your life.

THE TWO POLARITIES

All the signs are divided into two polarities, either masculine or feminine types. The male signs are more active and extroverted, as in the Chinese philosophical term yang, which refers to the positive, bright, and masculine. The female signs are considered more sensitive, meditative, and inward looking, as in the Chinese yin, which is the negative, dark, and feminine. Of course, astrology has always acknowledged that everyone embodies both female and male energies in their nature.

As a Virgo, your essence is feminine. You have strong female traits in your essential nature, which will interact with all the cultural and societal influences you encounter, as well as the other influences in your astrological chart (for instance, the location of the moon at your birth).

THE THREE QUALITIES

A lesser known aspect of astrology divides the signs into three types of qualities—cardinal, fixed, or mutable—which have to do with how you relate to the world. The four cardinal signs (Aries, Cancer, Libra, and Capricorn) are the most assertive and the most interested in making changes, leading, and being in control. The four fixed signs (Taurus, Leo, Scorpio, and Aquarius) tend to resist outside influences, and are strong and stable at best, or stubborn and perverse at worst.

As a Virgo, you are one of the four mutable signs, along with Gemini, Sagittarius, and Pisces. You are the most changeable and open to outside influences. The good news is that you can be adaptable and easy-going. The bad news is that you may tend towards instability or be easily dominated.

THE FOUR ELEMENTS

Each sign of the Zodiac is also associated with one of the four elements: fire, earth, air, or water, which lend certain characteristics to those signs. The three fire signs are Aries, Leo, and Sagittarius—they tend to be energetic, impatient, explosive and, well, fiery.

The three air signs—Gemini, Libra, and Aquarius—are the thinkers, the intellectuals, and the planners. They are all about ideas, thought, and speech, and are responsible for knowledge and communication on the planet.

The emotional water signs of the Zodiac are Cancer, Scorpio, and Pisces. These are the sensitive ones, the dreamers, and the spiritualists. They are capable of great depths of emotion and compassion.

You, Virgo, are one of the earth signs of the Zodiac, along with Taurus and Capricorn. These earthy types are—you guessed it—

down to earth. You tend to be practical, reliable, and cautious. Virgo is also potent and productive. You enjoy close contact with the earth, such as in gardening, at which you probably excel.

YOUR RULING PLANETS

According to ancient astrology, the sun and moon ruled one house each, and the five other known planets (Mercury, Venus, Mars, Jupiter, and Saturn) ruled two houses each. As they were discovered, the farther distant planets of Uranus, Neptune, and Pluto were added to the ancient system, resulting in some houses having a "secondary" ruler.

You, Virgo, are ruled by the planet Mercury, which is associated with all forms of communication, self-analysis, and understanding. While the influence of Mercury allows you excellent communication skills, it also brings restlessness to your nature, and a tendency to be overly critical.

Virgo is a feminine—nurturing, vulnerable—sign, and is likely to be modest, hardworking, introverted, and self-sacrificing. Remember, too, that Virgo is a mutable sign; you may want to check and see if you are allowing yourself to be exploited as you busy yourself with all your many tasks.

MIXING WITH THE OTHER ELEMENTS

Everyone relies on the support of the Earth signs (Taurus, Virgo, and Capricorn) for stability. Spending time with a friend who is also an Earth sign may be comforting, as you will appreciate each other's practicality, but may not be particularly stimulating.

The combination of Fire and Earth is very powerful. Your Fire sign friends (Aries, Leo, and Sagittarius) need you to help them carry out their enthusiastic ideas and keep them grounded, although they will tend to be impatient with your careful, analytical ways. You will enjoy their energy and fire, just don't try to restrict them too much, or there may be a volcanic eruption!

Although Air and Earth would not appear to mix particularly well, your Air sign friends (Gemini, Libra, and Aquarius) are stimulating company. You share particular empathy with Geminis, also ruled by the planet Mercury. You will be able to keep these friends grounded, and you will appreciate the inspiration of their quick intelligence and their excellent communication skills.

The Water signs (Cancer, Scorpio, and Pisces) are the dreamers and spiritualists of the Zodiac. These friends, while they will seem very impractical to you, will calm your nervousness and bring inspiration to your life. Their esoteric ideas moderate your solid practicality.

WHAT'S YOUR MOON?

The position of the moon at your birth exerts a strong influence on the basic elements of your Virgo personality. The house occupied by the Moon channels the expression of your personality in such areas as maternal qualities, domestic interests, and emotional needs.

For example, a moon in Leo brings some confidence to your fussy Virgo nature: as a parent, your Virgo enthusiasm will be complemented by the Lion's self-assurance, making you a less critical and more successful parent. In romance, a moon in Leo brings warmth and passion to the typical Virgo coolness. You may want to investigate how your sun sign is tempered by the other influences in your astrological chart—it's both entertaining and a rich source of imagery and meaning.

VIRGOS IN LOVE

In general, Virgos tend to be shy and careful when it comes to relationships. Your modesty and charm can make you a very attractive companion, although your fastidiousness may drive your partner crazy. At your best, you are reliable, intelligent, gentle, and affectionate. You might want to avoid people who bring out your possible tendencies to be nervous, fussy, and hypercritical of yourself—and them. Instead, find a partner who will give you confidence and security without taking advantage of you.

Take a look at the coupons in this book: they are designed to help you explore your compatibility with other signs, bring out your best traits, and help you with your worst. Have a great time exploring the wisdom of the stars!

the**Coupon**Collection™

SOURCEBOOKS, INC.®
NAPERVILLE, ILLINOIS

Since Virgo is practical and something
of a **PERFECTIONIST**, you prefer to know
what's happening well in advance.
Now's the time to start planning your
next vacation. Pick an appealing location
and start making reservations.

Since they love to plan and adore travel, a Gemini would make the perfect partner for vacation planning.

theCouponCollection™

Sourcebooks, Inc®
Naperville, Illinois

To enhance your Virgo **STABILITY** and
bring out some **CREATIVITY,** try making something
out of clay or go and paint pottery.
You'll find this soothing and centering.

An inventive
Aquarius can bring
out the best in the
earthy Virgo.

theCouponCollection™

SOURCEBOOKS, INC.®
NAPERVILLE, ILLINOIS

Your element is earth—you'll never feel so free
as when you're walking barefoot on the earth.
With this coupon, **TAKE SOME TIME OFF**
and go get in your element.

Virgos who hook up
with a Taurus,
another Earth sign,
will find themselves
in a relationship that
rocks.

theCouponCollection™

SOURCEBOOKS, INC.®
NAPERVILLE, ILLINOIS

Virgo's nervous energy can be **CALMED**
when coming into contact with a water sign,
so try bringing some of the coolness of water
into your life. On the next warm day,
go and splash in a pool or lake.

A compassionate and understanding Pisces can be just what Virgo needs for balance.

theCouponCollection™

SOURCEBOOKS, INC.™
NAPERVILLE, ILLINOIS

With this coupon, **INDULGE YOURSELF** with a swim or a run the next time you're feeling hypercritical. The activity will soothe you.

Virgo will find an
energetic friend in
Leo—here's someone
who can keep up with
you!

theCouponCollection™

SOURCEBOOKS, INC.™
NAPERVILLE, ILLINOIS

Bring a **LITTLE AIR** into your earthy existence—try wearing cool blues, green, and white.

Diplomatic Libra can
help keep a busy
Virgo calm and
organized.

theCouponCollection™

SOURCEBOOKS, INC.®
NAPERVILLE, ILLINOIS

To **GROUND YOURSELF** after a long day,
go to the beach and dig your toes into the sand.

The practical, down-
to-earth quality of
Taurus is very
comforting to a Virgo.

the**Coupon**Collection™

SOURCEBOOKS, INC.
NAPERVILLE, ILLINOIS

You're **FASTIDIOUS** and **CAREFUL** in your
approach—today's the day to tackle the details.
Clean out a closet, catch up on some
correspondence, or rearrange a cabinet.
You'll feel great when you're finished.

A fiery, enthusiastic Aries may be just what Virgo needs to help get that project completed.

the Coupon Collection™

SOURCEBOOKS, INC.®
NAPERVILLE, ILLINOIS

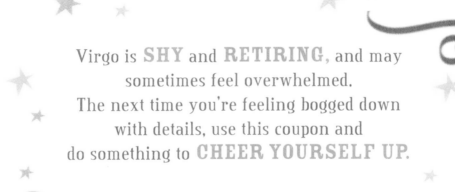

Virgo is **SHY** and **RETIRING**, and may sometimes feel overwhelmed. The next time you're feeling bogged down with details, use this coupon and do something to **CHEER YOURSELF UP**.

Virgo, find yourself
an optimistic,
freedom-loving
Sagittarius, and you'll
never stop having
fun.

theCouponCollection™

SOURCEBOOKS, INC®
Naperville, Illinois

Feeling stressed by everything you've taken on?
Try a balancing yoga posture like "tree."
Stand on one foot and bring your other foot up your leg,
all the way to the top of the inner thigh.
Open your knee and bring your palms together
in front of your heart in prayer position.
Breathe deeply until you can feel yourself lighten up.

Aquarians are naturally friendly and charming, and can bring Virgo a renewed enthusiasm for life.

theCouponCollection™

SOURCEBOOKS, INC.
NAPERVILLE, ILLINOIS

EXPRESS your Virgo spirit—wear a
neat new pair of high quality,
buttery soft leather gloves.

The esoteric, dreamy Pisces paired with the curious Virgo can find no end of imaginative, luscious fun.

theCouponCollection™

SOURCEBOOKS, INC®
NAPERVILLE, ILLINOIS 60567

Virgo is one of the most **PRODUCTIVE**,
robust, and fertile signs, even though
you have conservative tendencies.
Today's the day to enroll others in
a cause and **MAKE SOMETHING HAPPEN**.

The intense Scorpio is brilliant at pursuing a goal with almost obsessive tenacity—a quality that Virgos will want on their side.

theCouponCollection™

SOURCEBOOKS, INC.®
NAPERVILLE, ILLINOIS

For a few minutes of Virgo **PEACE**,
sit on the floor and close your eyes to meditate.

When an energetic Virgo and an inventive Aquarius get together, there's no end to what they can accomplish.

theCouponCollection™

SOURCEBOOKS, INC.™
NAPERVILLE, ILLINOIS

It will always make Virgo happy
to get in touch with the earth.
Go and work in your garden,
TAKING AS MUCH TIME AS YOU'D LIKE.

Earth signs Taurus
and Virgo share a
love of gardens and
an affinity for the
earth.

theCouponCollection™

SOURCEBOOKS, INC.®
NAPERVILLE, ILLINOIS

What could be more symbolic of Virgo nature
than **BALLROOM DANCING**?
Orderly and concise, but active.
Tonight's the night to go have fun until dawn.

A sunny, lively Leo
can make the perfect
dance partner for
Virgo—you won't
mind them taking the
lead, and they will
find you a reliable
and congenial
companion.

theCouponCollection™

SOURCEBOOKS, INC.
NASHVILLE ILLINOIS

Virgo is **INTROSPECTIVE** and **ANALYTICAL**.
This coupon gives you permission to
buy yourself a special journal and write
in it every day. Don't show it to anyone else!

Virgo and Gemini
share a gift for
excellent
communication skills.

theCouponCollection™

SOURCEBOOKS, INC.®
NAPERVILLE, ILLINOIS

The next time you need to get your **NERVOUS ENERGY** under control, this coupon entitles you to do some controlled yoga breathing. Sit back on your heels and blow the air out of your mouth as if you were blowing out a candle. With each exhale, pull the navel back toward the spine. Allow the inhale to be automatic and the belly to relax as you inhale. Do twenty breaths this way and then rest.

Virgo and the complex Capricorn are a match made in heaven—or is it earth?

theCouponCollection

SOURCEBOOKS, INC.
NAPERVILLE, ILLINOIS

Indulge that active Virgoan **CURIOSITY**—
spend an afternoon in the library
(control your urge to arrange the books
properly on the shelves).

Virgo and Sagittarius make a gregarious, congenial pair—Virgo's practicality balances Sagittarian carelessness, and Sagittarius' good humor complements Virgo's shyness.

theCouponCollection™

SOURCEBOOKS, INC.
NAPERVILLE, ILLINOIS

Splashing in puddles allows a Virgo
to feel carefree and young again.
GO FOR IT!

Find a free-spirited Gemini for a playmate. They are full of surprises, making them lots of fun to be around.

theCouponCollection™

SOURCEBOOKS, INC.
NAPERVILLE, ILLINOIS

All that Virgo perfectionism making
you feel frustrated? Go running or ride your bike
TO LIFT YOUR SPIRITS.

Hook up with one of your energetic Aries friends; they probably need to burn off some energy.

the**Coupon**Collection™

SOURCEBOOKS, INC.
NAPERVILLE, ILLINOIS

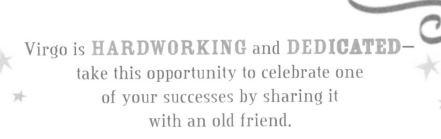

Virgo is **HARDWORKING** and **DEDICATED**—
take this opportunity to celebrate one
of your successes by sharing it
with an old friend.

A warm and earthy Taurus will remind a diligent Virgo to take time for sensual pleasures.

theCouponCollection™

SOURCEBOOKS, INC.
NAPERVILLE, ILLINOIS

You have an **ACTIVE INTELLIGENCE**
and **EXTRAORDINARY CURIOSITY**.
Sign up for a course in psychology
or religion and learn something more
about these important subjects.
See if a friend would like to join you.

The intellectual
Aquarius is always
interested in
discovering
something new, and
can help elevate
Virgo's ideas.

theCouponCollection™

SOURCEBOOKS, INC.®
NAPERVILLE, ILLINOIS

Cook a sumptuous meal and invite
your closest friends over to join you.
Bring out an expensive bottle of wine and
REFLECT ON LIFE.

That kind, sensitive
Cancer would love to
share a meal with a
Virgo friend, and
Cancer is the best
cook in the Zodiac!

theCouponCollection™

SOURCEBOOKS, INC.
NAPERVILLE, ILLINOIS

When you're feeling really flighty, **GROUND YOURSELF** by dressing in earth tones—dark green, warm brown, golden yellow.

The company of a
Capricorn can help
keep Virgo firmly
rooted in the Earth.

theCouponCollection™

SOURCEBOOKS, INC.®
NAPERVILLE, ILLINOIS

Your **MUTABLE NATURE** makes you want
to change things around—today,
just sit down in the middle of your living room
and enjoy the current furniture arrangement.
You can always change it again tomorrow!

Pisces understands a Virgo more than you might imagine. Both are mutable signs, finding it easy to let go, although Virgo needs more security than the mystical Fish.

theCouponCollection™

SOURCEBOOKS, INC.®
NAPERVILLE, ILLINOIS

Watery activities **COUNTERBALANCE** feelings of nervousness. Pick up some watercolors and paint a huge mural.

Get together with a Pisces for inspiration, a Leo to run the show, and a Gemini to help everyone communicate, while you, Virgo, will probably do most of the work!

theCouponCollection

SOURCEBOOKS, INC.
NAPERVILLE, ILLINOIS

The next time it rains, bring the water
and earth elements together to ground you—take off
your shoes and **WALK BAREFOOT**
in a mud puddle.

Fire signs (like Aries) rely on Earth signs like Virgo for practical support and Water signs for emotional support.

theCouponCollection™

SOURCEBOOKS, INC.
NAPERVILLE, ILLINOIS

Bringing fire into your environment
will enhance your ENERGY and enthusiasm.
Tonight, eat dinner by candlelight.
If you want to go all out,
light up the whole house with candles.

Tonight you might enjoy the company of a strong, golden Leo with a radiant personality.

the**Coupon**Collection™

SOURCEBOOKS, INC.
NAPERVILLE, ILLINOIS

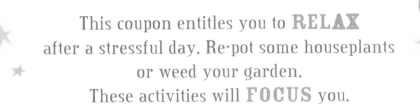

This coupon entitles you to **RELAX**
after a stressful day. Re-pot some houseplants
or weed your garden.
These activities will **FOCUS** you.

A mercurial Virgo
can help an intense,
introverted Scorpio to
open up, while the
Scorpio's dark
sensuality can bring
emotional depth to
the life of the modest
Virgo.

theCouponCollection™

SOURCEBOOKS, INC.
NAPERVILLE, ILLINOIS

Small animals such as rabbits and
domestic pets come under the rule of Virgo—if you're
not up for getting a **NEW KITTEN**, why not start
a collection of small ceramic
or gemstone rabbits or cats?

Signs of the Zodiac
have long been
associated with
certain gems, metals,
animals, flowers, and
even herbs and
spices.

theCouponCollection™

SOURCEBOOKS, INC.®
NAPERVILLE, ILLINOIS

Use your **HARDWORKING** character
to help someone else. Go and help a neighbor
or co-worker. They'll be grateful
to know that you care.

Virgo, you might want to team up with an idealistic Aquarius—you'll bring steady purpose to their humanitarianism, and their originality will inspire you.

theCouponCollection™

SOURCEBOOKS, INC.®
NAPERVILLE, ILLINOIS

Sometimes you take on too many duties.
This coupon entitles you to **PARE DOWN**
your To Do list to only a few items today.
Delegate or forget about the rest.

A powerful Leo can teach Virgo a great deal about tactful delegation and skillful organization.

theCouponCollection™

SOURCEBOOKS, INC.®
NAPERVILLE, ILLINOIS

To get you **CENTERED**,
do some sit ups.
Remember to breathe!

A gentle Libra can help you find all the balance and harmony you need in your life.

theCouponCollection

SOURCEBOOKS, INC®
NAPERVILLE, ILLINOIS

This coupon entitles you to **RELAX**
with a cup of steaming chamomile or peppermint tea—
good for the stomach complaints
that may trouble the Virgo.

Each Zodiac sign is said to rule a particular part of the body—Virgo rules the stomach and the nervous system.

theCouponCollection™

SOURCEBOOKS, INC.®
NAPERVILLE, ILLINOIS

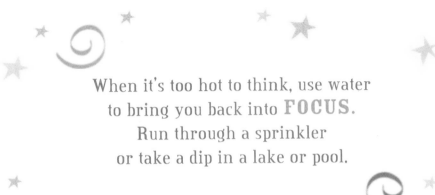

When it's too hot to think, use water
to bring you back into **FOCUS**.
Run through a sprinkler
or take a dip in a lake or pool.

Virgo will find the
company of a quirky
Pisces very
refreshing.

theCouponCollection™
SOURCEBOOKS, INC®
NAPERVILLE, ILLINOIS

This coupon entitles you to
EASE YOUR ANXIETIES for a minute.
If you feel yourself getting stressed,
take five deep breaths,
then go back to what you were doing.

Look to a charming
Taurus when you
want some peace and
comfort.

theCouponCollection™

SOURCEBOOKS, INC.™
NAPERVILLE, ILLINOIS

Because Virgo gets nervous when things are getting out of control, you may want to take stock of where you are and where you're going. This coupon entitles you to a **QUIET DAY** completing half-finished projects and making plans for new ones.

If you need help,
Virgo can always
look to the energetic,
enthusiastic Fire
signs or the bright,
intelligent Air signs.

theCouponCollection™

SOURCEBOOKS, INC.®
NAPERVILLE, ILLINOIS

Virgo, this coupon entitles you to
INDULGE YOUR LOVE OF DETAIL
by spending as much time as you like re-organizing
your closet, address book, or kitchen cabinets.
Go ahead and alphabetize that spice rack!

Nobody understands
Virgo better than
another Virgo—when
working together,
clarify responsibilities
so you don't tread on
each other's toes, and
you can be incredibly
productive!

theCouponCollection™

SOURCEBOOKS, INC.®
NAPERVILLE, ILLINOIS